ANIMAL FRIENDS OF THE SIERRA

By Fran Hubbard

Illustrated by William D. Berry

CONTENTS

Why Do We Have National Parks?	2	Facts About Feet	21
Who Are The Mammals?	3	California Ground Squirrel	22
The Mule Deer	4	Golden-mantled Ground Squirrel	22
The Black Bear	6	The Belding Ground Squirrel	23
The Mountain Lion	8	The Chipmunk	23
The Mountain Coyote	10	The Gray Squirrel	24
The Bobcat	12	The Chickaree	24
The Gray Fox	12	The Yellow-haired Porcupine	25
The Raccoon	13	Tracks Tell Tales	26
The Ring-tailed Cat	13	The Beaver	27
The Striped Skunk	14	The Marmot	28
The Spotted Skunk	14	The Woodrat	28
The Long-tailed Weasel	15	The Deer Mouse	29
The Sierra Pine Marten	15	The Meadow Mouse	29
When Winter Comes	16	The Pika	30
The Bats	18	The Pocket Gopher	30
The Flying Squirrel	19	The Cottontail	31
The Shrew	20	The Jackrabbit	31
The Mole	20	The Sad Tale of Blackie Bear	32
Teeth Are Like Tools	21		

YOSEMITE

LASSEN

SEQUOIA

KINGS CANYON

WHY DO WE HAVE NATIONAL PARKS?

THE RANGER NATURALIST was talking in the shade of a big yellow pine tree, where the group was resting during their nature walk. "Do you know", he began, "there are four national parks in California—more than in any other state in our country? To the north, where the Cascade Range meets the Sierra, is Lassen Volcanic National Park. It contains the only active volcano in the United States. Near the center of the Sierra is Yosemite, with its beautiful valley and high waterfalls. Kings Canyon, the next, is famous for its mountain wilderness. Sequoia National Park is the farthest south. It was named for the oldest living things in the world—the giant sequoia trees which are protected there. These wonderful parks belong to us—to you, to me, and to all Americans. We should be proud of them."

A boy interrupted to say, "What do you mean, they 'belong to us.' Do I own one?"

The ranger smiled and pushed back his stiff-brimmed hat. "Son, the national parks have been set aside by our Congress—the Congress of the United States—and by the President, for all of us. Here you and your parents, and someday your children will always be able to see what our country was like before the white man came. We have many people now, and we have made many changes in the land. With our big cities and our super-highways and our dams, before long there just won't be much wilderness left. But we will always have wilderness in our national parks. They will be places where you can go to rest and enjoy the beautiful mountains and lakes and trees like this big pine we're under. All of them are just the way they were hundreds of years ago, except for the roads and trails and camps that have been made to help you enjoy them. Maybe you are more interested in seeing the birds and animals—"

Another boy asked, "Do you have mountain lions in this park?" "Sure do," the ranger replied. "We have many kinds of animals here, and they are all being protected so that you can see and enjoy them."

"Well, could you tell us about some of them—the big ones I mean?"

The ranger smiled and said, "I'd be glad to. When you say 'the big ones' you must mean the mammals, like the bear and the deer. Do you know what a mammal is? It's a warm-blooded animal with a backbone. It has hair on its body and gives milk to its young."

A mouse - -

A man - -

An elephant - -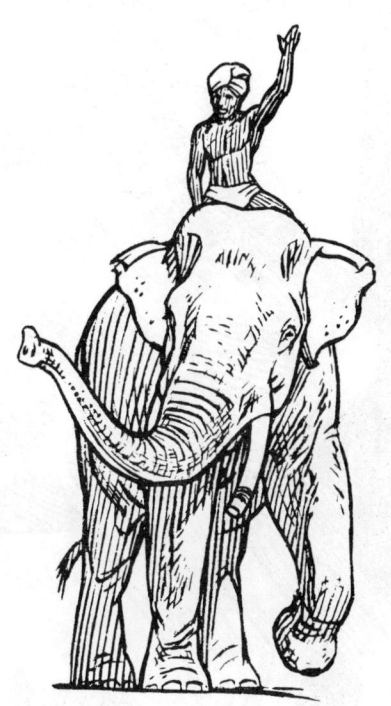

And even a whale--

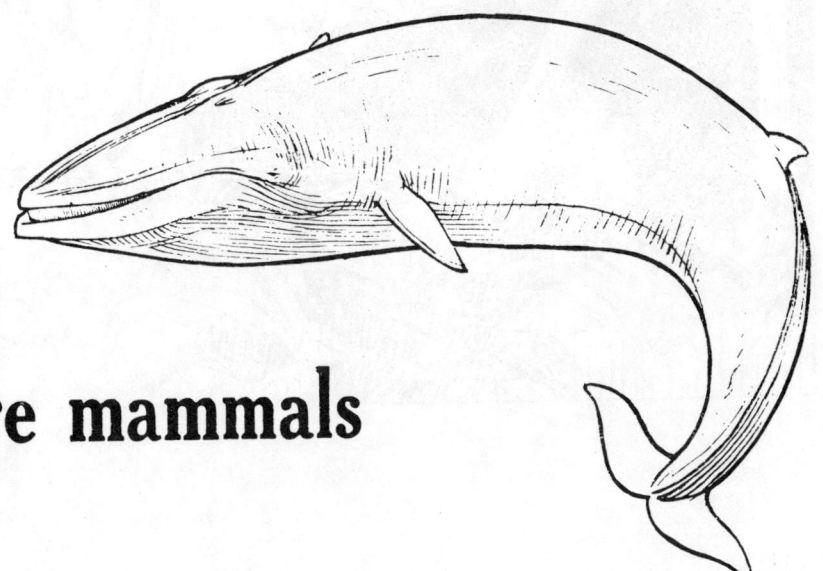

All are mammals

*Let's talk about some of
the mammals of California*

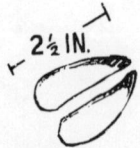

THE MULE DEER

One of the most beautiful of our Sierran mammals is the California mule deer. He was named for his large, mule-like ears. They are always in motion. When he is alarmed they are erect and forward, facing the possible danger. When he is angry his ears are flattened sideways. When he is hiding they are sometimes laid back against his neck.

The babies, called fawns, are born in late May and early June. Often there are twins or even triplets. The mother doe hides the fawns to keep them safe. They know that they must not move until she calls them. Their reddish coat with its white spots blends well with the forest thickets. This is called "protective coloration" and is their only defense during the first weeks of their lives. If you find a fawn that is hidden do not touch it. Its mother has not forgotten it. If you give it a human smell from your hands you will make it easier for some animal-enemy to find it. By the time they are about four months old many of the fawns lose their spots and no longer require their mothers' milk.

Deer are browsers. This means that much of their food is made up of twigs, buds, and leaves. They are also fond of acorns and grass. Because of danger from mountain lions and other enemies the deer gobble their food quickly into a special part of the stomach. Then they chew it later in some safe place, the same way a cow chews its cud.

The male deer, called a "buck," grows antlers. His antlers are not like the horns of cattle, because they are shed each winter and a new set grown in the spring. A young buck grows an extra point each year but it is not possible to tell his exact age by counting them. This is because in later years fewer points grow. Bucks use their antlers for fighting during the mating season. Once they drop off, discarded antlers form an important source of bone-building food for the small creatures of the forest. Next to man, the mountain lion is the greatest enemy of the deer. Deer can run swiftly for speed is their main protection from enemies. Coyotes and bobcats will sometimes hunt them too. Mother deer show great bravery when their fawns are in danger. They will even charge full-grown coyotes and make them run. Tame and friendly as the deer may seem in our national parks you must remember that they are still wild animals. Their front hoofs are sharp and they strike swiftly and without warning. Visitors who don't understand about wild animals are injured every year while feeding and petting deer. They feed the deer things they shouldn't eat, and this of course makes them sick. It's fun to watch the deer from a safe distance, but only a greenhorn tries to feed and pet them.

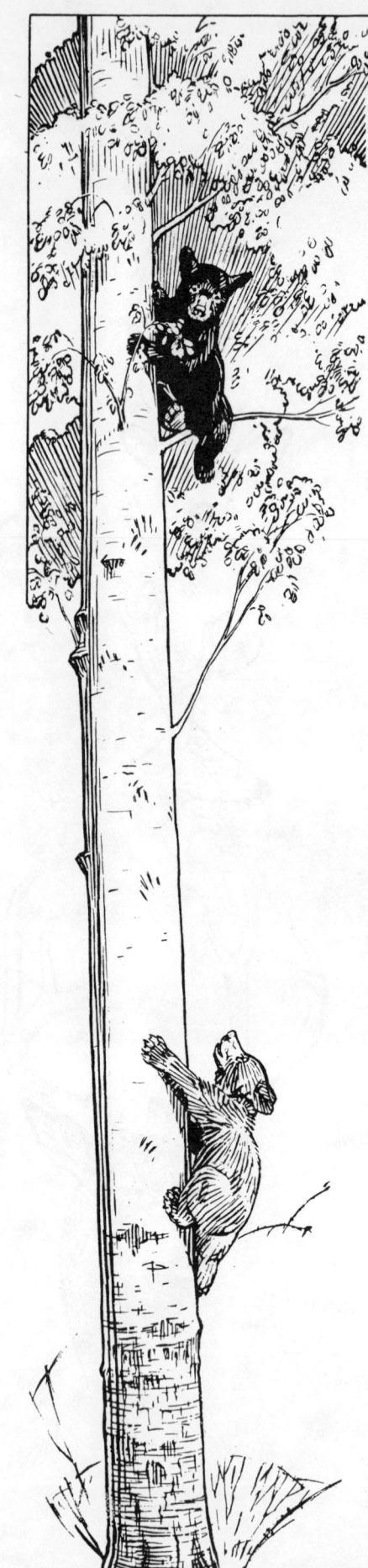

THE BLACK BEAR

Black bears are not always black. Just as people have hair of different colors, so it is with bears. They are most often brown, but many are black. Some are the color of straw and we call them "cinnamon bears". Black bears are found throughout the entire Sierra. Now that the grizzly bear is gone they are the largest fur-bearing mammals in California. They usually weigh between 200 and 300 pounds, but some have been known to weigh as much as 500!

Bears usually travel with a clumsy, plodding walk, but when alarmed or angry they can move like greased lightening. Their tracks are easily recognized. Unlike the dog or cat, the front paws leave different tracks from the back ones (see illustration). These animals are good climbers and often scramble up a tree when they are frightened. Instead of coming down head-first, bears back down. Their hearing and smell are good, though their eyesight is poor.

Bears are so big that they have few natural enemies. Of course they try to avoid skunks and porcupines, but once in a while a young bear gets porcupine quills in himself.

Bears are omnivorous, (om-niv-or-us) which means they will eat almost anything, and they seem to always be hungry. They like to eat many kinds of plants and animals but they seldom kill for themselves. Much of the meat they eat has been killed by others. Sometimes a bear develops a taste for livestock but fortunately this does not happen often.

Animals have their own highways. The forest floor is covered with paths made by different creatures as they carry on their daily lives. You may have trouble finding a mouse trail but a bear trail is easy to identify. In many places the shuffling of thousands of bear feet has worn a path deep into the ground.

Many people think bears hibernate, (hy-bur-nate, or sleep soundly) all winter. They do have a long sleep in winter, at least in the higher mountains, but they may be awakened easily and sometimes come out to hunt for food. It is during the winter sleep of the mother that the young are born. She usually has twins although one or three are not uncommon. The little ones stay in the den until they are about three months old. When the cubs leave the den the mother guards them carefully. At the first sign of danger she gives a barking grunt and chases them up a tree. She is strict and the cubs soon learn that they must mind or be spanked. They stay with their mother for the first year while she teaches them. All bears should be let alone, but a mother bear with cubs is the most dangerous. Since all animals are protected in our national parks, many bears have lost their natural fear of man. But like the deer, they should be treated as wild animals, and never fed or petted.

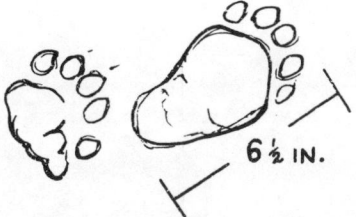

THE MOUNTAIN LION

Probably the most misunderstood mammal in the Sierra is the mountain lion. These big cats range from Canada to South America but are seldom seen. They have a great fear of man, so men have little reason to be afraid of them. They have seldom been known to attack people. Lions are carnivores (car-nih-vores—that means "meat-eaters") and they like deer best. But they will eat bobcats, raccoons, and even skunks. In some cases where lions have become cattle-killers, it was found that they were old or crippled and could not catch their natural food.

In many ways mountain lions are like big, overgrown housecats. Their tracks are similar though many times larger, and they can move as silently. When hunting, one may creep along with his belly almost scraping the ground, or he may crouch, motionless except for a twitching of the end of his long tail. These cats have a variety of names. They have been called "panther", "cougar", "catamount", "painter", and "puma", but the name "mountain lion" probably describes them best.

For a den the mother lion often chooses a cave among the rocks. This makes a good home for the babies. Her two or three kittens are usually born in the springtime, but they may come at any season. The little ones have black spots on their yellow-brown coats and black stripes on the tops of their long tails. As they become older, longer fur grows in and covers the baby spots. By the time they are a year old they take on either the reddish-brown or the grayish-brown of their parents. Like all kittens, baby mountain lions are playful and the mother often romps with them.

Except for man, the mountain lion apparently has few enemies. Sometimes he bothers a porcupine and gets some quills that cause infections.

3½ IN.

These cats are quiet, but they may utter a low growl, a hiss, or make a high, whistling sound. You may have heard stories about the scream of the mountain lion. Naturalists who have studied them believe that about 99 percent of the screams are actually made by other animals.*

Mountain lions play an important part in nature. By feeding on deer they prevent the deer from becoming too numerous. You aren't likely to see a mountain lion in the wild. But it is good to know that here in the national parks they are being protected. Now they will not become extinct (ek-stinkt — that means "gone forever") like the grizzly bear and plains wolf from California.

*You may learn more about mountain lions by reading *The Furbearing Mammals of California*, by Grinnell, Dixon and Linsdale, volume 2.

THE MOUNTAIN COYOTE

Have you ever heard a coyote sing? Coyotes are great singers. In the mountains or on the desert they may often be heard, filling the air with their strange music. The song often starts with a series of short barks followed by a long, mournful howl. Two or three coyotes can sound like twenty. Naturalists believe that they not only enjoy their song, but also use it as a means of calling and signalling to one another. Since there are no more wolves in California, coyotes are the largest native dogs. Their tracks look like a dog's with the toenails showing.

Coyotes like variety in their dens. Sometimes they dig long tunnels with many branches and rooms. Other times they enlarge a hole made by some other digging animal. A cave among the rocks may be used for a home. One coyote family may have different dens—one for daytime naps, one or more for nurseries, and one for the father coyote when the mother is taking care of the pups. As they grow older, the pups dig little burrows of their own in the sides of the main den.* There usually are about six young in a litter, born in April or May. Though their eyes are closed and they are helpless when they are born, coyote puppies develop quickly. At an early age they learn to hunt for themselves. By the time they are six months old they are as big as their parents and are on their own. Coyotes are the most widely-known carnivores (remember that word?—meat eaters) in California. They eat hundreds of thousands of rodents each year, including ground squirrels, mice, and gophers. Sometimes they learn to like chickens or sheep but many ranchers protect them because they keep their pastures free of ground squirrels and other destructive animals. They are crafty hunters. Two will sometimes work together. One trots out in plain sight to attract the attention of the animal they are hunting while the second, which has kept hidden, sneaks up quietly from behind. They have sharp eyes, good hearing, and a keen sense of smell. All of these help them in hunting. In California we have three kinds of coyotes — the mountain, valley, and desert types. Of the three, mountain coyotes are by far the most beautiful. Living in higher, colder country makes their fur grow thick and long, and the tail is furrier. Sometimes they are called "gray wolf" or "timber wolf" because of their large size. Except for man, they have few enemies. Mother deer have been known to charge and strike them with their hoofs when they came too close to their fawns, and young coyotes have been injured by quills from porcupines. Coyotes may often be seen in the Sierra, hunting in mountain meadows or trotting along trails in the forest. If you should hear them howling don't be afraid—remember that they are really singing and are thoroughly enjoying themselves!

2½ IN.

*More about the family life of the coyote is told by Ernest Thompson Seton in volume 1, page 371 of his *Lives of Game Animals*.

THE BOBCAT

The bobcat looks much like a housecat, except for his pointed ears and short, bobbed tail. Most carnivorous animals hunt at night, but the bobcat also likes to forage (hunt food) in the daytime. Like all cats he sometimes catches birds, but he feeds mostly on ground squirrels, mice and other harmful rodents. These cats are found throughout California but there are fewer in desert regions than in the mountains. The kittens are born in the springtime. The mother does not allow other animals, including the father bobcat, to come near. Though they don't really feel at home in trees, bobcats will climb when in danger. The creatures of the forest are often warned of a bobcat's approach by the screeching of the jays and other birds.

THE GRAY FOX

If you are lucky sometime you may see a gray fox running along the road. They are nocturnal, (noc-tur-nal) which means they are most active at night. Then is when you may catch a glimpse of one prowling through underbrush in search of rodents and other food. Gray foxes like to eat plants, but meat makes up more than half of their diet. Baby foxes are called "kits" and are born in March or April, often in a den among rocks or in a hollow tree. By the time they are five months old the kits are big enough to leave their parents. Gray foxes like to climb trees. This is unusual for members of the dog family.

THE RACCOON

Raccoons love water. One of their scientific names means "one who washes", because they carefully wash their food whenever they can. They are omnivorous and eat all sorts of things. Much of their food is found around their homes near the water. The front paws are like tiny hands and they use them well. This, combined with a great curiosity, sometimes makes the raccoon destructive when kept as a pet. Like bears, raccoons walk flat-footed and their tracks are easily recognized (see page 21). The young come in the springtime and there may be from three to seven of them. There are only two California mammals having ringed tails—the raccoon and the ring-tailed cat. You will know the raccoon when you see him by his robber-like mask.

THE RING-TAILED CAT

In gold rush days the ring-tailed cat was often called "miner's cat" because miners kept them as pets to catch rats and mice. Rodents are their favorite food but they also like birds and berries. Ring-tails live in almost all parts of the Sierra, but are seldom seen because they are active only at night. Their bright eyes are large, to help them see in the darkness. The beautiful black and white banded tail is more than just an ornament. Not only does it help him in balancing when he climbs but it is used to keep him warm. He tucks his head beneath his chest and wraps his warm tail about him, becoming a fluffy ball of fur.

THE STRIPED SKUNK

Almost everyone avoids the skunk. This handsome black and white animal defends himself with a bad-smelling fluid sprayed from small pockets beneath his tail. However, this means of defense is used only as a last resort. Skunks first stamp their front feet and try to frighten the other animal away. Most of his hunting is done at night, and insects make up more than half of his food. Holes among the rocks and hollow logs in brushy woods make natural homes for them. The babies are born in the springtime and the mother soon teaches them to hunt. Perhaps someday you will see a parade of baby skunks walking single-file behind their mother as they all go in search of food.

THE SPOTTED SKUNK

Spotted skunks are much smaller than their striped relatives. They do all of their hunting at night. Meat and insects are their favorite foods but they will eat many other things. Their means of protection is the same as the striped skunk's except that they do an interesting "handstand" as they spray. The great horned owl, the eagle, and the mountain lion are among the few animals that dare to hunt skunks. Spotted skunks are sometimes called "civet cats" but this name is not correct. Stories are told about skunks biting dogs and giving them rabies (or hydrophobia). Rabies are no more common among skunks than among many other wild and domestic animals. With their insect-eating habits, skunks are among the most valuable wild mammals in California.

THE LONG-TAILED WEASEL

The long-tailed weasel is well equipped for his way of life. His "streamlined" body makes it possible for him to move with great speed and to squeeze through narrow places. In summer his light yellow and tan coat blends well with the dry grass. In winter he becomes pure white except for his black-tipped tail. This white fur is often called "ermine". He is a killer. Most small animals and birds fear him and with good reason, for he will attack an animal much larger than himself. The weasel has few enemies but sometimes meets his equal when attacking a large snake. Mice and other rodents are a favorite food and for this reason weasels are useful animals to have around.

THE PINE MARTEN

Perhaps in the high forests of the Sierra you may see a golden-brown, cat-like animal leaping gracefully through the trees. This creature with the bushy tail is the Sierra pine marten. Like his cousin the weasel, he is always on the move; but unlike the weasel he is as much at home in trees as among the rocks. He is so light on his feet that he can move through the forest and leave scarcely a trace. In winter a thick covering of hair grows on the pads of his feet. This makes a kind of snowshoe so travel is easier across soft snow. Small rodents make up most of his food, but he sometimes eats birds. His worst enemy is man, who hunts him for his fur, called "American sable".

Have you wondered what animals do

The pika works hard all summer harvesting and storing plants which will be his winter food. When snow covers the ground he remains active in his cozy home.

When the winds blow cold the chipmunk curls up in his warm nest to sleep until the spring sunshine wakes him.

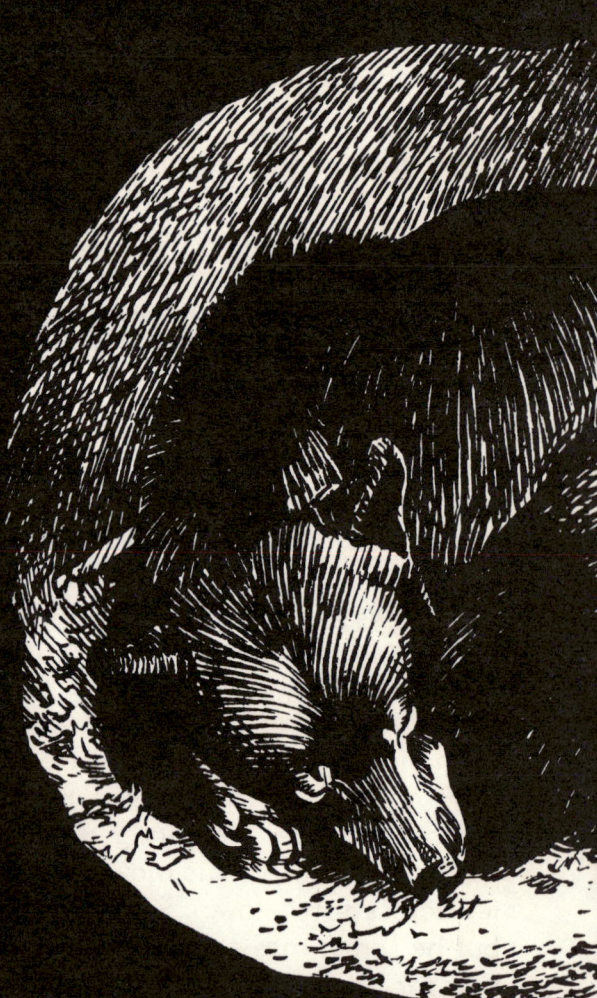

Bears don't really hibernate. They sleep during the winter but awaken easily if something disturbs them.

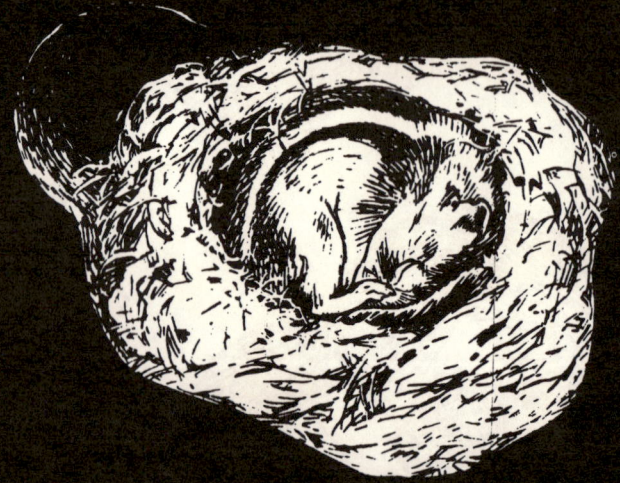

The California ground squirrel sleeps twice during the year. In addition to his winter hibernation he also sleeps during the heat of the summer. This summer sleep is called "estivation".

WHEN WINTER COMES

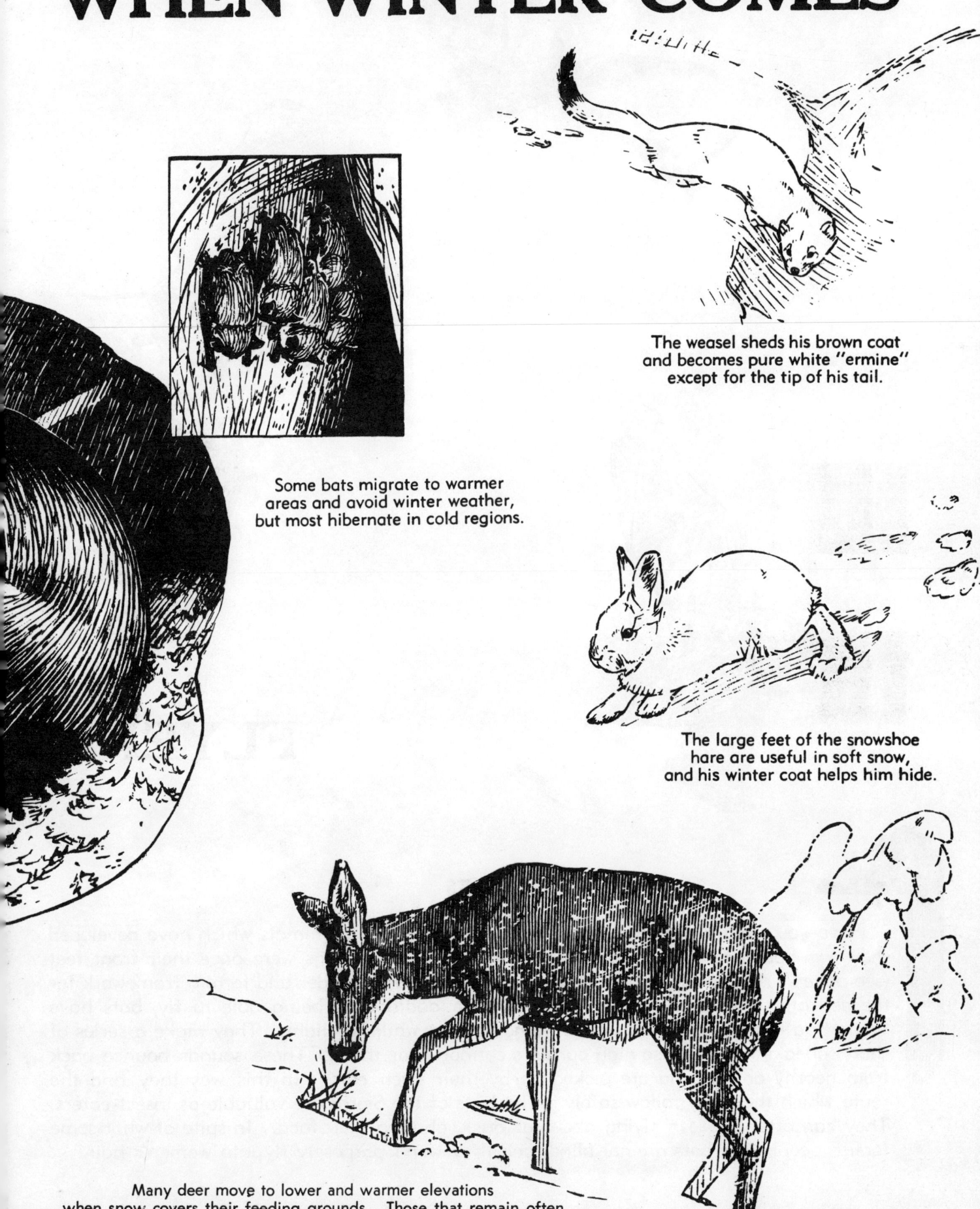

The weasel sheds his brown coat and becomes pure white "ermine" except for the tip of his tail.

Some bats migrate to warmer areas and avoid winter weather, but most hibernate in cold regions.

The large feet of the snowshoe hare are useful in soft snow, and his winter coat helps him hide.

Many deer move to lower and warmer elevations when snow covers their feeding grounds. Those that remain often have to paw through deep snow to find food.

FLYERS

BATS

Have you ever wished that you could fly? The only mammals which have developed their own bodies for flying are the bats. What are now wings were once their front feet (see page 21). The finger bones have become long and slender and form a framework for the delicate membrane (skin) of the wing. In addition to being able to fly, bats have "radar", a remarkable means of avoiding objects while in flight. They make a series of short squeaks which are so high our ears cannot hear them. These sounds bounce back from nearby objects and are picked up by their keen ears. In this way they find the route which they may follow safely. The bats of the Sierra are valuable as insect-eaters. They can often be seen flying about at dusk, chasing their food. In spite of what some foolish people say, bats are not blind, and they won't purposely fly into women's hair.

GLIDERS

THE FLYING SQUIRREL

Flying squirrels don't really fly—instead they glide. At each side of their body is a loose fold of fur-covered skin. When they are ready to glide they leap into space from high up in a tree, spreading their legs. The loose skin is tightened like a sail, and they glide gracefully down, usually to the base of a nearby tree. Their furry tails are flat like feathers and help in balancing and steering. Like most creatures of the night these little rodents have soft, smooth fur and large, bright eyes. They are light gray above and almost white on the underside. An old woodpecker hole makes a favorite nesting place and they like many kinds of foods. Owls are their worst enemies but members of the weasel family hunt them too. Flying squirrels are seldom out during daylight but in the light of your campfire sometime you may see a flash of white overhead as one sails by.

THE SHREW

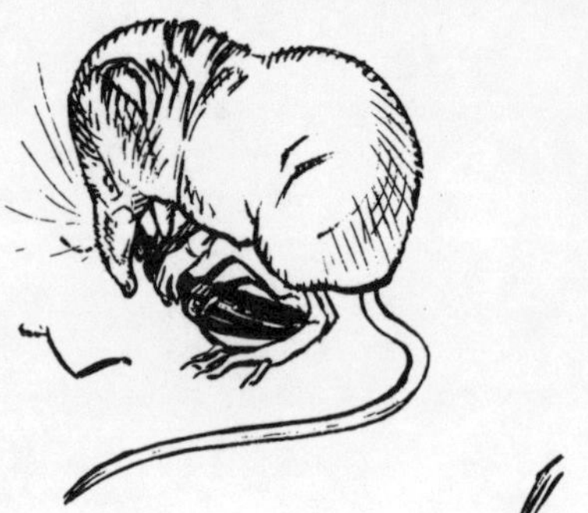

We have talked about the black bear—our largest fur-bearer in the Sierra, now let's talk about the smallest—the shrew. He is not only the smallest in the Sierra but shrews are the smallest mammals in the world. The easiest way of recognizing the shrew and telling him from a mouse is by the long snout. It's a good thing that shrews are small, for they are sharp-toothed and vicious and have been known to eat twice their own weight in meat in just a few hours. In California shrews live from dry deserts to damp streamsides. One variety, the water shrew, has even learned to run across the surface of the water.

THE MOLE

The mole is built for an underground life. Because he nearly always stays in his burrow we seldom see him. He finds everything he needs beneath the earth. You can tell where a mole is at work by the ridge of dirt which he pushes up as he forces his way along. Unlike the gopher, he is strictly a meat-eater and feeds on earthworms and insects. His gray fur is soft and he has a short, stubby tail. Moles do have eyes but since they spend their lives in the dark eyes are of little use. His front legs are strong and the broad front feet have long, heavy claws for digging. You can see how this helps him in his life down below.

Teeth Are Like Tools

Mammals' teeth are well adapted to their different ways of life. We might compare them to common tools. Rodents have front teeth which are sharp and shaped like chisels. They are for gnawing. Carnivores such as cats can only tear and shred with their sharp teeth. Moles and shrews have many fine, pointed teeth used for gripping like a trap or a pair of pincers. The deer family have large, flat molars which are used for grinding. Our teeth are a combination of these.

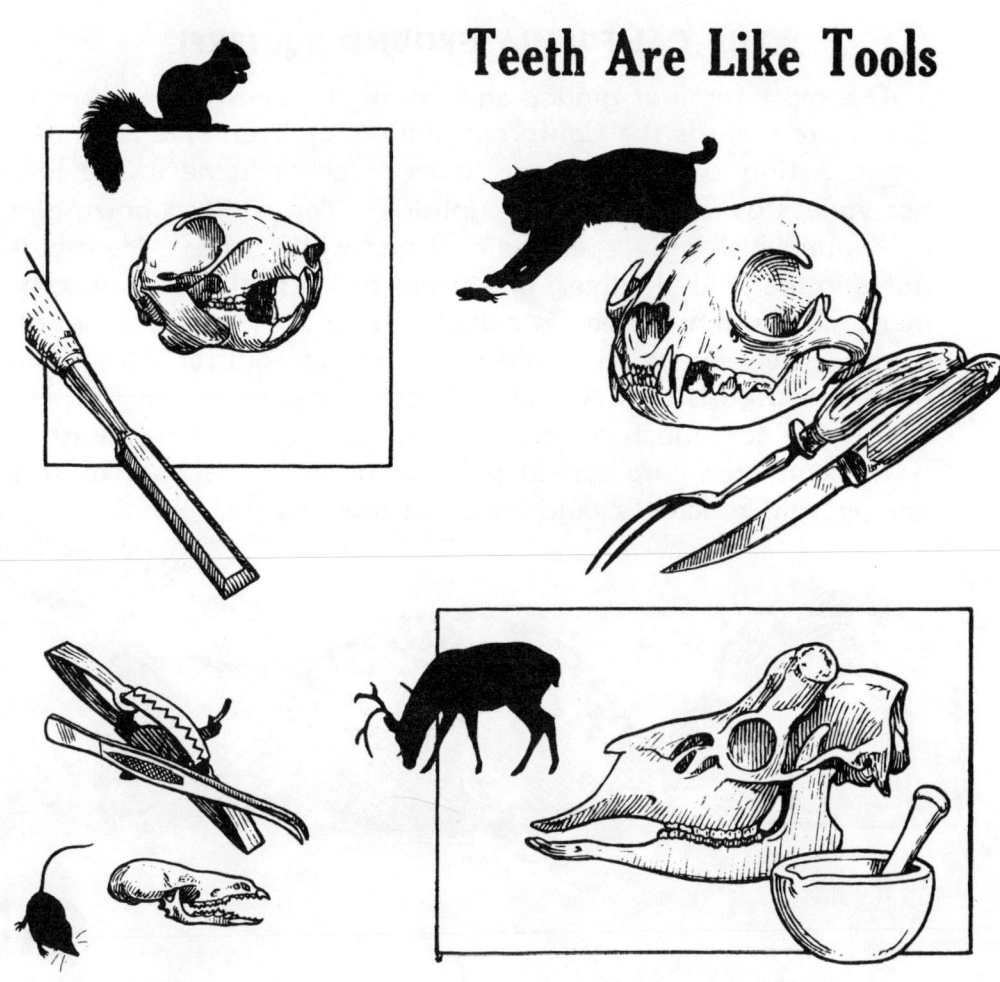

Facts About Feet

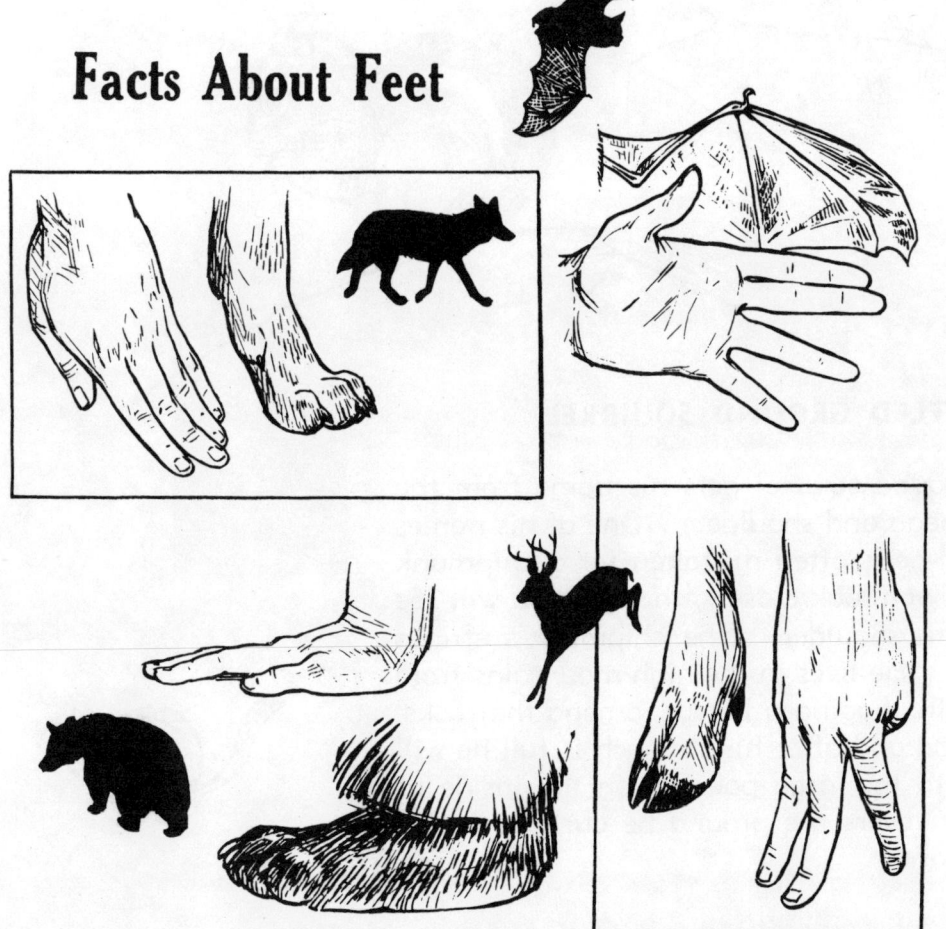

Now let's talk about the different kinds of mammal feet. We might see how they resemble our own hands. The wing of the bat can hardly be called a "foot" but it has developed from a foot. Many of the bones are similar to the bones of our hands. Members of the dog family walk on what would be the first and second joints of our fingers, while deer walk on two fingertips. Bears and raccoons are flat-footed and walk palm-down.

THE CALIFORNIA GROUND SQUIRREL

The most familiar ground squirrel in the Sierra as well as in the entire state is the California ground squirrel. He is omnivorous, eating everything, and is as much at home in the low, hot valleys as in the cooler mountains. You will recognize him by his brownish-gray, speckled coat and white collar. He hibernates in the cold of winter, and sleeps again in the heat of summer. This summer sleep is called "estivation" (es-tih-va-shun). In wilderness areas the California ground squirrel does some good because his burrows help prevent soil erosion. In farming country he does much damage. Fleas carried by ground squirrels have been known to spread bubonic plague. Because of this danger wild rodents should never be touched.

GNAWERS

GOLDEN-MANTLED GROUND SQUIRREL

The golden-mantled ground squirrel gets his name from the reddish-gold color of his head and shoulders. One of his names is "calico chipmunk" and he is often mistaken for a chipmunk because of his stripes. If you look closely, though, you will see that the stripes end at his shoulder. The chipmunk's stripes run to the end of his nose. He lives in the high mountains from 6,000 to 8,000 feet, usually digging a burrow among the rocks. He eats many kinds of food and after his stomach is full he will continue to cram food into the large pouches on the inside of each cheek. When snow covers the ground he curls up in his snug burrow to sleep all winter.

THE BELDING GROUND SQUIRREL

Sometime when you are in the high country you may hear the shrill, chattering voice of the Belding ground squirrel. This small, tan creature has little fear of man. He has an appealing habit of sitting erect and perfectly still, with front paws resting on his chest. When he sits like this he looks like a picket pin, a short stake used for tying horses in the early days. So he was named "picket pin" by early travelers, and is called by that name today. He lives almost entirely on grass and plant foods. Like other ground squirrels the picket pin hibernates during the winter. Because winters are long in the high Sierra, he spends more of his life asleep than awake!

THE CHIPMUNK

One of the busiest workers in the forest is the chipmunk. Although he sleeps about half of the year, he makes up for lost time in the summer. He is as much at home in trees as on the ground, and often makes a snug nest in the hollow of a tree trunk. If you come too close to his home he will scold loudly. Up with the sun, he goes about collecting seeds and berries. What he doesn't eat is tucked away in the two cheek pouches. When these are full he digs a hole and buries the food for later use. Sometimes he forgets where he has hidden them and some of the seeds grow. Without knowing it the chipmunk is a conservationist, (con-sur-vay-shun-ist), helping replant the forest.

THE GRAY SQUIRREL

"Shadow-tail" describes the gray squirrel so well that it was chosen for one of his scientific names. His fluffy gray tail is as long as his body, and it is useful as well as beautiful. Much of his life is spent in the trees so the tail helps balance while climbing and jumping from branch to branch. He is often a target for "dive-bombing" by acorn woodpeckers, and again the tail proves its usefulness—he protects himself by spreading it over his body. Acorns and seeds are among his favorite foods, and like the chipmunk he often buries them. The gray squirrel does not hibernate in winter, but when the weather is cold or stormy he stays in his warm nest high in the trees.

THE CHICKAREE

"Give him wings and he would outfly any bird in the woods." John Muir used these words to describe the chickaree, the little red tree squirrel who is the clown of the forest. Never still a moment, he bounds from one tree to another, pausing only to scold some intruder with his shrill, chattering voice. It is not a good idea to walk under the trees when he is at work, for he cuts down dozens of green pine, fir, and sequoia cones. Many of these he stores in damp places for his winter food. He knows the seeds will not fall out when the cones are wet. The chickaree is active all winter and you will often see him scampering across the snow.

THE PORCUPINE

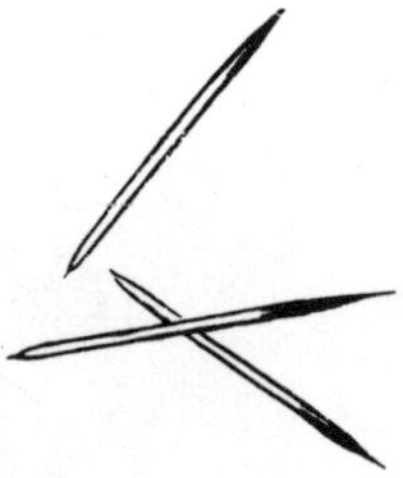

The porcupine is just about the most unsociable creature in the woods. He feels so safe, with his large supply of sharp quills, that he ignores everyone about him. Through the ages these quills have developed from hairs. On his head they are about an inch long and on his back they grow to four inches. When danger is near he puffs himself up until he is almost twice his normal size. This makes his quills stick straight out from his body. He doesn't really throw his quills as many people think he does. He lashes his prickly tail back and forth, striking at the enemy. Each quill has a sharp point and hundreds of tiny barbs which make it work farther into the victim. With this kind of ammunition it's no wonder that the other animals stay out of his way! The porcupine doesn't hibernate in winter, although he often lives in snow country. He is herbivorous (er-biv-or-us) which means he eats plants, and he feeds and travels both in the daytime and at night. His big appetite often makes him do damage. Trees are sometimes killed when he eats too much of their tender, inner bark. Tools are also damaged when he eats the wooden handles, perhaps for the salt flavor. Slow-moving porky has a reputation for being stupid, but he is useful to have in the forest. People lost and without food have been able to save their lives by killing and eating porcupines.

Tracks Tell Tales

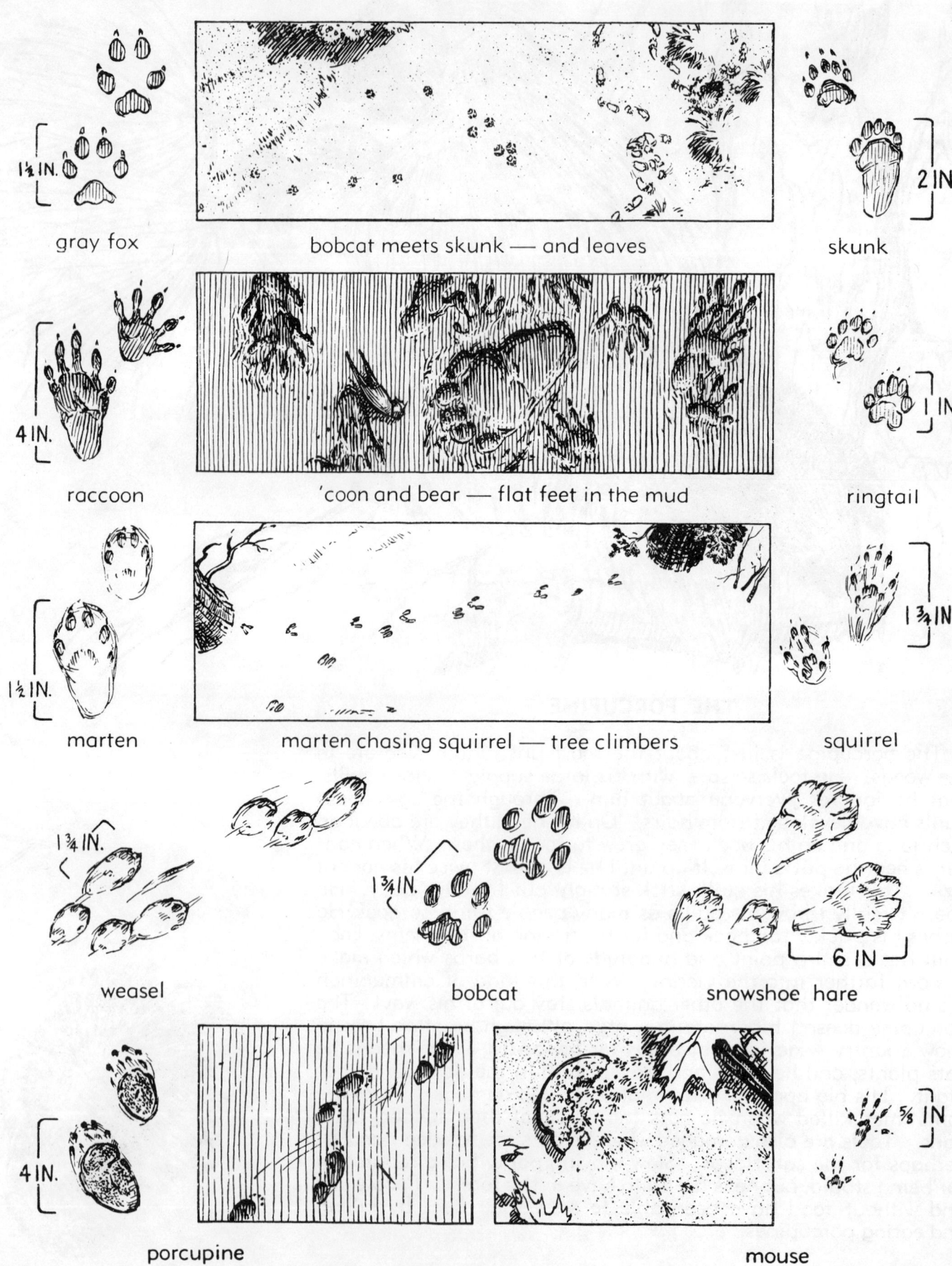

gray fox • bobcat meets skunk — and leaves • skunk

raccoon • 'coon and bear — flat feet in the mud • ringtail

marten • marten chasing squirrel — tree climbers • squirrel

weasel • bobcat • snowshoe hare

porcupine • mouse

THE BEAVER

The beaver does not rightly belong to the Sierra because he was moved here from lower country by man. But since he is here, let's talk about him. His most interesting feature is his scaly, flat tail. It not only helps him steer when he is swimming but by slapping it on the surface of the water he sounds the alarm of an enemy's approach. When he stands on his hind legs to gnaw a tree he uses his tail as a brace. He is an expert swimmer and like all good swimmers he makes no noise. To help him swim the toes of his hind feet are webbed like a duck's (see illustration).

The beaver is the largest rodent in California and often weighs more than 40 pounds. Rodent's front teeth are not like ours. They continue to grow as they are worn down. Even if a tooth is broken it grows back within a few days. This is important to the beaver for his teeth are his tools and without them he would die.

In early days our West was explored by trappers searching for beaver pelts (fur). The beaver has beautiful, soft, thick fur because he spends his life in the water. The beavers build most of their dams at night, to form ponds deep enough to hide the underwater entrances to their homes in the streambanks. They make them of trees and branches cut on the stream's edge. Water in the ponds soaks into the earth, keeping the meadows green.

THE MARMOT

A neighbor of the Belding ground squirrel and the pika is the yellow-bellied marmot. His home is high in the Sierra, where he digs a burrow among the rocks. Because he reminds people of his eastern relatives he is often called a woodchuck or ground hog. He loves the sun and when the weather is warm he spreads out on a rock for a sunbath. If his enemy the eagle flies near he warns the countryside with a shrill whistle. He is a plant-eater, and living near the Sierran meadows, food supply is no problem for him. All summer long he eats so that when winter comes he is so fat he can crawl away into his burrow to hibernate until spring.

THE BUSHY-TAILED WOODRAT

"Pack rat" or "trade rat" are the names by which most of us know the woodrat. Shiny things catch his eye and he will often pack them away. If he is already carrying something he may drop it for the new treasure, which makes people say that he is "trading". Unlike the rats in cities, he has a bushy tail and his gray and white coat is neat and clean. Night time is when the woodrat hunts for food. His home is among the brush or in the rocks and is made of sticks with a grassy nest inside. Because he is always adding sticks to his house it becomes a real fortress. By the time his enemies dig into the nest the woodrat is far away.

THE DEER MOUSE

The deer mouse is one of the cleanest of all the forest creatures. Before his eyes are even open, the baby deer mouse learns to wash his face. He sits up, licks his front paws, and washes with both at once. He is very different from the dirt-carrying mice of the city. His coat is brown with white underneath. His feet are also white, so he is sometimes called the white-footed mouse. He is active at night and his eyes are large to help him find his way in the dark. Perhaps a deer mouse will visit you sometime when you are camped in the woods. He likes your kind of food as well as the seeds upon which he usually feeds.

THE MEADOW MOUSE

Our mountain meadows are often criss-crossed with hundreds of grassy tunnels. These are the work of the meadow mouse. Much of his daily business is carried on in the runways where he is not so easily seen by his enemies. If you watch quietly you may see him darting through the grass. He is a stubby, grayish-brown creature with a blunt nose and a short tail. He looks very much like a small gopher. His nest is made of finely chopped grasses and may be hidden under a log or rock. When many of the forest animals are hibernating the meadow mouse stays awake. He may not see the sky all winter for he is busy making runways and looking for food beneath the snow.

THE PIKA

"Little Chief Hare" is the name that the Indians gave the pika, or cony. Even though his ears are small and round and his tail is so little it can hardly be seen, he belongs to the rabbit family. In rock slides of the high Sierra, families of pikas live together. During the spring and summer he harvests piles of grass and other plants. These are heaped into "haystacks" for drying. He is active all winter, and when his home is buried beneath many feet of snow he has plenty to eat. We usually think of rabbits as being silent. The pika has a shrill voice which can be heard a long way. He uses it as a warning signal if danger is near.

THE POCKET GOPHER

There are thousands of pocket gophers in the Sierra, but probably you have never seen one. This is because the gopher spends almost all of his life under the ground. He has strong front feet, like the mole, with long claws for digging. He can close his lips behind his front teeth to keep dirt out of his mouth as he digs or cuts roots. His tail has sensitive hairs near its tip, which tell him where he is going when he moves backward. He is a vegetarian (plant-eater) and on either side of his mouth he has a pouch or pocket in which he carries food (see illustration). In winter he makes tunnels through the snow, and fills them with dirt from his burrows. When the snow melts these dirt cores are left to tell the story of his winter's work.

THE COTTONTAIL RABBIT

Down in the foothills lives the little cottontail. He gets his name from his fluffy white tail which looks very much like a ball of cotton. His light gray coat helps him hide among the brush where he has his burrow. All of his life may be spent in the same thicket, with its network of small paths. Here the babies are born in a nest lined with fur which their mother has pulled from her own coat to keep them warm. The cottontail can't rely upon speed alone for protection. Instead he doubles back on his own trail or "freezes". And when he does "freeze" he stays so completely motionless that he can hardly be seen at all.

THE BLACK-TAILED JACKRABBIT

The jackrabbit's long ears reminded some old-timer of a jackass, and there he got his name. But he isn't really a rabbit at all. He is a hare. The difference between the two is that hares can hop about at birth, their eyes are open, and they have fur. Baby rabbit's eyes are closed, they have no fur, and they are helpless for more than a week. The mother jackrabbit makes no nest for her babies. Instead, after they are born she hides each one in a place by himself, returning at night to nurse him. The jackrabbit eats plants and lives in the open. He depends upon his sharp eyes and ears for warning, and upon the speed of his long legs for safety.

The ranger naturalist looked at his watch. "We haven't talked about all of the animals in the Sierra, today. Maybe we can tell you about more of them another time. But before we go let me tell you about Blackie the Bear. Blackie got into trouble one day, with the help of some park visitors:

Blackie was a good bear until one day the picnickers discovered Blackie.

then Blackie discovered the picnic—

and tried to keep it for himself.

So everyone called him a bad bear. He was trapped and taken far away, where there were no people and no picnics. But Blackie never understood. He had only helped himself to a bear's share, as any bear will when invited to lunch.

DON'T FEED THE BEARS!

Author's Note: Our thanks go to the teachers who offered helpful suggestions and encouragement during the preparation of this book.